# BUTTERFLIES

# Butterflies

# Butterflies

Butterflies have long captured the imaginations of humans. Perhaps this is due to the fact that they lend a splash colour or blur of brightness to a sunny day, or to the amazing transformations they undertake during the course of their lives, switching from egg to caterpillar to chrysalis to winged adult butterfly.

The thousands of butterfly species include many rare ones that are have tiny ranges and highly specific habitat requirements, from alpine meadows to dense rainforests, while others are much more generalist and range widely over

large areas and can be found in back yards
and even city parks.

    With butterflies commonly found in
most habitats and most parts of the world,
our fascination has been borne out over the
millennia with these special insects frequently
featuring in the art and literature of many
cultures. This beautiful book combines gorgeous
watercolour paintings and other artworks of
butterflies with quotes about nature and life in
general, from the deep and meaningful to the
light hearted and frivolous.

"*Try to be a rainbow
in someone's cloud.*"

– MAYA ANGELOU

"*The sun is simple.*
*A sword is simple.*
*A storm is simple.*
*Behind everything simple*
*is a huge tail*
*of complicated.*"

– TERRY PRATCHETT

"*Be faithful in small things because it is in them that your strength lies.*"

– MOTHER TERESA

"This is the room where
Jezebel frescoed her eyelids
with history's tragic glitter."

– TOM ROBBINS

"Let the blue sky
   meet the blue sea
   and all is blue
   for a time."

– MONCY BARBOUR

*"True strength is delicate."*

– LOUISE NEVELSON

"Admiral. That part
of a warship which
does the talking while
the figurehead does
the thinking."

– AMBROSE BIERCE

"*It was with deep interest that my companion and myself, both now about to see and examine the beauties of a tropical country for the first time, gazed on the land where I, at least, eventually spent eleven of the best years of my life.*"

– HENRY WALTER BATES

"*Blessed are they who see beautiful things in humble places where other people see nothing.*"

– CAMILLE PISSARRO

"A season of loneliness
and isolation is when the
caterpillar gets its wings.
Remember that next time
you feel alone."

– MANDY HALE

"*Without butterflies, the world would soon have few flowers. There is enough room in the sky for all flyers.*"

– TRINA PAULUS

"*Blue colour is everlastingly appointed by the deity to be a source of delight.*"

– JOHN RUSKIN

"*Nothing is pleasant that is not spiced with variety.*"

– FRANCIS BACON

"*I only ask to be free.*
    *The butterflies are free.*"

– CHARLES DICKENS

"Alone we can do so little;

*together we can do so much.*"

— HELEN KELLER

"*What's a butterfly garden without butterflies?*"

– ROY ROGERS

"*Painting is just another way of keeping a diary.*"

– PABLO PICASSO

"*Let the little fairy
in you fly!*"

– RUFUS WAINWRIGHT

"The secret of happiness is variety, but the secret of variety, like the secret of all spices, is knowing when to use it."

– DANIEL GILBERT

*"Be like a peacock
and dance with
all of your beauty."*

– DEBASISH MRIDHA

"We have buried so much of
the delicate magic of life."

– D. H. LAWRENCE

"As she fled fast
   through sun and shade,
The happy winds
   upon her play'd,
Blowing the ringlet
   from the braid."

– ALFRED LORD TENNYSON

"*The essence of
the beautiful is
unity in variety.*"

– WILLIAM SOMERSET MAUGHAM

"*I fear that we are
such gods or demigods
only as fauns and satyrs,
the divine allied to beasts,
the creatures of appetite,
and that, to some extent,
our very life is our disgrace.*"

– HENRY DAVID THOREAU

"*I have lived long enough to witness the vanishing of wild mammals, butterflies, mayflies, songbirds and fish that I once feared my grandchildren would not experience: it has all happened faster than even the pessimists predicted.*"

– GEORGE MONBIOT

*"Just living isn't enough,"*
*said the butterfly,*
*"one must have sunshine,*
*freedom and a little flower."*

– HANS CHRISTIAN ANDERSON

"*Butterflies can't see their wings. They can't see how truly beautiful they are, but everyone else can. People are like that as well.*"

– NAYA RIVERA

*"Look past your thoughts,*
*so you may drink*
*the pure nectar*
*of this moment."*

– RUMI

*"Spring is
nature's way
of saying,
'Let's party!'"*

– ROBIN WILLIAMS

"Great things are done
  by a series of small things
  brought together."

– VINCENT VAN GOGH

"To learn
one must be humble.
But life is the great teacher."

– JAMES JOYCE

"It is difficult to see
  why lace should be
  so expensive;
  it is mostly holes."

– MARY WILSON LITTLE

"*The butterfly counts
not months but moments,
and has time enough.*"

– RABINDRANATH TAGORE

"Name me an emperor
who was ever struck
by a cannonball."

– CHARLES V

"*Just because there's tarnish on the copper, doesn't mean there's not a shine beneath.*"

– LAURENCE YEP

"*Everyone is like a butterfly, they start out ugly and awkward and then morph into beautiful graceful butterflies that everyone loves.*"

– DREW BARRYMORE

"*Be it known that we, the greatest, are misthought.*"

– CLEOPATRA

"*The man who has no imagination has no wings.*"

— MUHAMMAD ALI

"*Literature and butterflies are the two sweetest passions known to man.*"

– VLADIMIR NABOKOV

*"The world is a looking glass
and gives back to every
man the reflection of his
own face."*

– WILLIAM MAKEPEACE THACKERAY

"I saw the angel
in the marble
and carved
until I set him
free."

– MICHELANGELO

"*Red is the ultimate cure for sadness.*"

– BILL BLASS

"*The beautiful spring came; and when Nature resumes her loveliness, the human soul is apt to revive also.*"

– HARRIET ANN JACOBS

"The caterpillar does all the work, but the butterfly gets all the publicity."

– GEORGE CARLIN

"*Life is a tiger*
*you have to grab by the tail,*
*and if you don't know*
*the nature of the beast*
*it will eat you up.*"

– STEPHEN KING

"*Feet, what do I need you for when I have wings to fly?*"

– FRIDA KAHLO

"*Nature's message was always there and for us to see. It was written on the wings of butterflies*"

– KJELL BLOCH SANDVED

"There is a sun, a light that
for want of another word
I can only call yellow,
pale sulphur yellow,
pale golden citron.
How lovely yellow is!"

– VINCENT VAN GOGH

"*Perhaps the butterfly is proof that you can go through a great deal of darkness yet still become something beautiful.*"

– BEAU TAPLIN

"*Everything has beauty,*
*but not everyone sees it.*"

– CONFUCIUS

"I dreamed I was a butterfly,
flitting around in the sky;
then I awoke.
Now I wonder:
Am I a man who dreamt
of being a butterfly,
or am I a butterfly
dreaming that
I am a man?"

– ZHUANGZI

"*Yellow is vagueness and luminousness, both.*"

– ALEXANDER THEROUX

"*Things are not quite so simple always as black and white.*"

– DORIS LESSING

"You can't depend
on your eyes
when your imagination
is out of focus."

– MARK TWAIN

"*Don't waste your time chasing butterflies. Mend your garden, and the butterflies will come.*"

– MARIO QUINTANA

"When I ran, I felt like a butterfly that was free."

– WILMA RUDOLPH

"*The words of Mercury are harsh after the songs of Apollo.*"

– WILLIAM SHAKESPEARE

"Let us live for the beauty
of our own reality."

– CHARLES LAMB

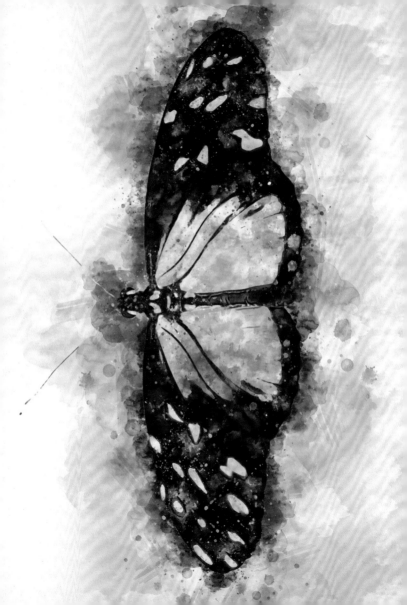

"The nectar of life is sweet
only when shared
with others."

– ADAM MICKIEWICZ

"Green is the prime colour
of the world, and that from
which its loveliness arises."

– PEDRO CALDERON DE LA BARCA

"*Orange is red brought nearer to humanity by yellow.*"

– WASSILY KANDINSKY

Published in 2023 by Reed New Holland Publishers
Sydney

Level 1, 178 Fox Valley Road, Wahroonga, NSW 2076, Australia

newhollandpublishers.com

A record of this book is held at the National Library of Australia.

ISBN 978 1 92107 364 9

Managing Director: Fiona Schultz
Publisher and Project Editor: Simon Papps
Designer: Andrew Davies
Production Director: Arlene Gippert
Printed in China

10 9 8 7 6 5 4 3 2 1

OTHER TITLES BY REED NEW HOLLAND INCLUDE:

*A Guide to Insects in Australia* (Fourth Edition)
Paul Zborowski and Ross Storey
ISBN 978 1 92554 607 1

*Butterflies of the World*
Adrian Hoskins
ISBN 978 1 92151 733 4

*Reed Concise Guide: Butterflies of Australia*
Paul Zborowski
ISBN 978 1 92554 694 1

*Insects of the World*
Paul Zborowski
ISBN 978 1 92554 609 5

*A Field Guide to Butterflies of Australia*
Garry Sankowsky and Geoff Walker
ISBN 978 1 92151 788 4

For details of these books and hundreds of other Natural History titles see newhollandpublishers.com and follow ReedNewHolland on Facebook